Don't change

In Jesus' Briefcase

Business Essentials for Missional Leaders

Written by: Stephen Rosenberger

In Jesus' Briefcase

Business Essentials for Missional Leaders

Copyright © 2011 WORD Solutions

Author: Stephen Rosenberger

Foreword by: Matt Anderson

Cover and Artwork by: Alyssa Bream

Edited by: Cindy Metzger

ISBN: 978-1463644956

Scripture taken from the HOLY BIBLE, NEW INTERNATIONAL VERSION. Copyright 1973, 1978, 1984, 2011 by International Bible Society. Used by permission of Zondervan Bible Publishers.

FOREWORD

We love formulas – hard-and-fast rules that work in every situation. I suppose it is part of our fallen nature to long for predictability in a world where answers can be difficult to find. When we watch the news and see the plight of many nations in turmoil or hear about economic malaise in our own country, we find odd comfort in a + b = c. We like knowing that some things always work. Our boss may have shown up to work in a bad mood this morning, making our day miserable, but it's still, "I before E except after C." Our kids may be showing all the signs of making bad personal choices, and we cannot do a thing about it. However, we can always count on the fact that, "30 days have September, April, June, and November." The stock market may be down, but when we're using a screwdriver it's always, "Lefty Loosey, Righty Tighty." We abhor volatility, and in our continual state of flux, it is nice to know there are things we can always count on.

In the church world, we love formulas just as much. In dealing with the heart and soul of people (What can be more unpredictable than that?), we church folk have this nasty habit of seeing something work on one occasion and implementing it for every successive occasion. Today's emergency caulking and duct tape repair can become tomorrow's Spackle Ministry. A successful drama or musical presentation can become so inherently sacred ten years later that to even suggest a different one elicits threats of excommunication. In short, today's solution can easily become tomorrow's idol.

In Numbers 21, when the Israelites spoke against God, the Almighty sent venomous snakes as penalty. Realizing their sin, they cried to Moses who prayed to God on their behalf. God immediately proposed a remedy. "The Lord said to Moses, 'Make a snake and put it up on a pole; anyone who is bitten can look at it and live.' So Moses made a bronze snake and put it up on a pole. Then when anyone was bitten by a snake and looked at the bronze snake, they lived" (Numbers 21:8-9, NIV). God provided a specific answer for a specific problem. But the people mistook the fix for a formula. We find that hundreds of years later, King Hezekiah "...removed the high places, smashed the sacred stones and cut down the Asherah poles. He broke into pieces the bronze snake Moses had made, for up to that time the Israelites had been burning incense to it (It was called Nehushtan.)" (II Kings 18:4, NIV). The snakes were long gone, but the pole remained. They had even named it. The tool had become an object of worship. It is amazing how we in the church can confuse methodology with mission.

If we are honest with ourselves, we have to admit that we have a few "Nehushtans" of our own in the 21st century church. We are often more passionate about certain church programs than personal evangelism. We demand our kids experience all the same denominational rites of passage we enjoyed and quickly forget that God already laid out a scriptural blueprint for reaching humanity with the Good News of His death and resurrection. Rather than bowing before the Lord in order to hear His voice for this generation, we opt for the bronze snake that "brought about that great healing crusade many years ago". Certain songs must be sung with certain instruments led by people in a certain wardrobe. Certain events must happen whether they are useful or not. After all, it is the 22nd Annual Flea Market and Chili Cook-off. But outside of God's directive, we're burning incense to inanimate objects.

Stephen Rosenberger's new book, "In Jesus' Briefcase" appeals to a grand, scriptural simplicity. He dares leaders to a needed inventory of their organizational heart to see if we are fulfilling the commands of Christ to the Church's first generation. In reading Stephen's book, I was reminded of how difficult I have often made the business of church. I become so enamored with flowcharts and feeding the organizational machine that I forget about feeding the poor and hungry right around me. It is a necessary wake-up call to eliminating the unnecessary and emphasizing the scriptural. New churches will see it as a road map to their congregation's formation. Existing churches will need it to expose the bronze snakes that have crawled through the hidden crevices of their assembly. I pray that you will have the courage to implement the principles in this book, rather than simply dismissing it as mere idealism. Maybe you can take these concepts and begin to initiate an organizational revival in your church. Maybe you can team up with other leaders on your board or staff to be the change agent that brings about a renaissance to your house of worship. Remember: if it is scriptural, it is possible. Allow this book to be the impetus that brings about new life.

Let us dispense with our spiritual formulas and come back to what makes God smile – hearing and obeying His voice. "In Jesus' Briefcase" will be a great place to start. Happy reading!

-Matt Anderson

CONTENTS

Introduction 2

Section 1: *Marketing*

Chapter 1: Marketing Basics 6

Chapter 2: Embracing Innovation 18

Section 2: *Leadership*

Chapter 3: A Leader Worth Following 28

Chapter 4: Finding Value in the Body 32

Chapter 5: Empowering People 42

Section 3: *Operations*

Chapter 6: Organizational Cultures 52

Chapter 7: Stewardship 58

Chapter 8: A Freely Giving Church 72

Chapter 9: An Organization Re-made 78

ACKNOWLEDGMENTS

Dedication:

This book is dedicated to every individual who has thrown caution-to-the-wind and sacrificed freedom, privilege and creature comforts to pursue *the call* of God. More than anyone else, they understand organic missiology as it was meant to be implemented by every believer in Christ Jesus. May this book provide the slightest glimpse into how the Church can return to operating the same way.

Thanks:

To anyone and everyone who has poured into me: thank you from the bottom of my heart. I've often stated that there has never been a person I met who didn't impact my life in some manner: so to all I've encountered in this life: thank you. My family and friends whose constant love and support motivates me to accomplish more today than I did yesterday: thank you. Colleagues along the way who inspired me to be better than in days before: thank you. Most of all I must acknowledge my Lord and Savior Jesus Christ who saved me from a life of sin and its resulting damnation: thank you!

INTRODUCTION

In Jesus' Briefcase is designed to offer a fresh perspective on the integration of sound business principles in the church. Whether you're a senior leader within the organization or a part of the network of volunteers facilitating its ministries, this book was created for you!

Historically the distance between the marketing, leadership and operations strategies of churches versus other organizations has been vast. *In Jesus' Briefcase* is written to close that gap in as much as Scripture permits. In fact, it is my firm belief that God's Word is a complete blueprint for living in this world: that includes how we perform as non-profit organizations.

Admittedly, I cannot help where my heart is on matters of the Church: I am more passionate about its origins than I have ever been before. Supposing that each one of us can identify significant turning points in our life, mine is a transformation that has rudely awakened me to the deepest needs of my brothers and sisters. My faith has been challenged and my world has been unequivocally shattered into pieces through an exploration of the true paradigm for ministry: Scripture.

It seems as though the incredibly organic ministry of Jesus is the only model worth following, so that's what I long to practice, teach and write about. You'll find that throughout this text each and every business principle is drawn from Scripture, calling us to manage our organizations in the Spirit-inspired, early New Testament way.

Why must we pursue our ecclesiological roots? In our efforts to become established churches (or Para-church organizations), many of us have missed how to be the actual Church. Let's face it; the years have not been kind to the church. We've fended off scandals of all kinds, many involving the misappropriation or embezzlement of funds. Others just simply don't trust the way we manage resources, lead people or interact with the marginalized in our community.

As a body of believers in Christ, we must be more aware of the kind of business our church is doing because the world is watching closely: what are our business practices telling them about us?

SECTION ONE

MARKETING

CHAPTER ONE

MARKETING BASICS

The Premise

We as believers in Christ have made the act of evangelism, or the marketing of God's love, much too complex when it's intentionally simple by design. I've imagined for some time that there's a reason why both pastors and used car salesmen are equally drawn towards the same unattractive polyester suits: not the kind that distinguished professors wear with leather patches on the elbows, but the kind that were purchased when the Cleveland May Company department store closed its doors. The material found in these suits isn't the only common thread between their occupants, for many have reduced the communication of the Gospel message to a methodical and passionless sales pitch.

The great commission, however, provides the church with an alternative to a sales-oriented marketing strategy. Jesus delivers these words:

> All authority in heaven and on earth has been given to me. Therefore go and make disciples of all nations, baptizing them in the name of the Father and of the Son and of the Holy Spirit, and teaching them to obey everything I have commanded you. And surely I am with you always, to the very end of the age.[1]

I've often stood amazed at the sheer number of statistics involved with the conquests of church growth; from attendance to baptisms, and tithe checks to the ever-important number of salvations. But in our effort to mass-market the Gospel are we compromising the integrity of the message? Churches count salvations and call it growth

---

[1] Matthew 28:18-20 (NIV)

when we see John and Sarah Smith return to the altar to accept the free gift of salvation in Christ for the third time this year alone. So what's the problem with the marketing strategy?

When we hone in on getting an individual to commit to a product through means of a high-pressure sales pitch, the chances of buyer's remorse are greater. Thus we have product on the shelves returned by consumers and salvation numbers on paper that don't exist in real life. The good news is that fixing this problem is simple, stop thinking of clever things to pitch to people to get them to 'come to the Lord' this Sunday, and more about loving them so much that they find their way there naturally. It's the Holy Spirit's job to convert, not ours. Remember, the great commission calls us to make disciples, not quick converts.

The Product

Effective marketing strategies probably aren't the first things that come to mind when trying to describe a thriving church, but they are paramount to its success. Every physical attribute to the church speaks to is esthetic appeal, and it's typically the esthetics that will initially attract the consumer; but will it keep them coming back for more?

I'm reminded of a beautifully crafted Mexican-American restaurant in my hometown that draws crowds by the busload. Every facet of the restaurant's Spanish-inspired exterior, from the stone tiles to the stucco walls, tells the passersby that this is a good place to find authentic cuisine: unfortunately, appearances are often deceiving. It was some of the most tasteless food I had ever consumed, and needless to say I won't be returning.

Having a great storefront is one thing, but if you offer a sub-par product nobody will come back to your beautifully crafted church building. Regardless of esthetics, the church still offers the greatest product available to mankind: the love of God through Christ Jesus! How could we as the church ever thought it could be a cozy coffee bar in the foyer, professional sounding musicians on the platform or the sweet breeze of an industrial strength air conditioner offering refreshment on a hot Sunday morning. Without the life changing power of love, your church may be esthetically pleasing, but spiritually void. 1 Corinthians 13 offers a familiar vantage point to the preeminence of love:

> If I speak in the tongues of men and of angels, but have not love, I am only a resounding gong or a clanging cymbal. If I have the gift of prophecy and can fathom all mysteries and all knowledge, and if I have a faith that can move mountains, but have not love, I am nothing. If I give all I possess to the poor and surrender my body to the flames, but have not love, I gain nothing.[2]

The Pitch

Now that we've established what our product is (love), how do we as the Church best market it? If we look to the ultimate marketing strategist of love for guidance, we shouldn't look any further than Jesus. Jesus marketed love by disassembling traditional methodology and

---

[2] 1 Corinthians 13:1-3 (NIV)

contextualizing the Gospel message to His audience.[3] He made the Gospel simple enough to be accessible to all.

So how might the application of that look today? I imagine not much different than it did some two thousand years ago. It seems as though the key is simplifying your organization. When you simplify you look less like a threat and disarm your audience; and let's face it, Jesus was a tycoon in the business of disarming people.

Disarming Strategy #1 – Know Your Customer

Who hasn't had the experience of either purchasing a product from a large retailer or addressing an issue with an overgrown service provider? You feel like a number, not a name. Unfortunately, that's one of the major downfalls to larger organizations; it's easy to lose touch with your customers. Over time the customer feels neglected and unrewarded for his/her loyalty, while the organization loses interest because an intimate relationship no longer exists between the two.

So how can we be better know our customers? Simple: engage people! Not in the shallow way by which we say hello on Sunday mornings as if we are actually family, or ask 'how are you' without regard for the answer, but in a truly genuine way that can only be driven by a heart full of compassion. Jesus knew His customer base, and developed a very organic style of engaging people. Bring to remembrance the story of the woman caught in adultery.

---

[3] Contextualizing the Gospel message refers to a process through which the message is communicated to an audience (large or small) by using social practices and language they would understand and use daily.

The teachers of the law and the Pharisees brought in a woman caught in adultery. They made her stand before the group and said to Jesus, "Teacher, this woman was caught in the act of adultery. In the Law Moses commanded us to stone such women. Now what do you say?" They were using this question as a trap, in order to have a basis for accusing him. But Jesus bent down and started to write on the ground with his finger. When they kept on questioning him, he straightened up and said to them, "If any one of you is without sin, let him be the first to throw a stone at her." Again he stooped down and wrote on the ground. At this, those who heard began to go away one at a time, the older ones first, until only Jesus was left, with the woman still standing there. Jesus straightened up and asked her, "Woman, where are they? Has no one condemned you?" "No one, sir," she said. "Then neither do I condemn you," Jesus declared. "Go now and leave your life of sin."[4]

Jesus could have very easily allowed this woman to be condemned to death; she was guilty of the offense. Instead, He chose the path of resistance for the sake of saving a life. Without truly answering the question, and fully knowing the Pharisees were attempting to trap Him through any definitive answer provided, Jesus elected to respond in a way that captured the hearts of all present. The Pharisees knew they were too guilty to stone, and the woman now knew the grace of God. Jesus knew the hearts of His audience that day, and acted accordingly.

When was the last time we as believers in Christ chose the path of greatest resistance? Each day we pass the same

---

[4] John 8:3-11 (NIV)

homeless man on our way to work without consideration for his life. He may be one missed meal away from eternity, but how will we know if we fail to engage him? Moreover, how will he hear of Christ if no one speaks the words of truth to him?

Disarming Strategy # 2 – Be Selective with Your Support Staff

Jesus didn't surround himself with well-educated, influential people: just average folks who were empowered to do extraordinary things. I can't imagine that anyone would have felt threatened by the presence of some dirty fishermen, so that's exactly who Jesus chose to use. God's selection process is different than ours.

> Brothers, think of what you were when you were called. Not many of you were wise by human standards; not many were influential; not many were of noble birth. But God chose the foolish things of the world to shame the wise; God chose the weak things of the world to shame the strong.[5]

This is not a case against education; in fact a solid education can only enhance one's ability to minister the Word of God. What we're establishing here is that God can use whatever He chooses to accomplish His purposes. As ministers it is our job to recognize the move of God outside the confines of what we would traditionally expect (i.e. the most educated).

---

[5] 1 Corinthians 1:26-27 (NIV)

Disarming Strategy #3 – Level the Playing Field

Potentially, the greatest reason for atheism in our world today is the hypocrisy of many churchgoers. Why? We're all perpetual failures, just some saved by grace. The Apostle Paul explains in the very familiar passage: "for all have sinned and fall short of the glory of God."[6]

By leveling the playing field, we tell the unbeliever that we are sinners, saved by grace, in pursuit of sanctification.[7] Essentially, we are communicating that we are no better than the vilest sinner.

> For by the grace given me I say to every one of you: Do not think of yourself more highly than you ought, but rather think of yourself with sober judgment, in accordance with the measure of faith God has given you.[8]

Those with an aversion to Christianity only become defensive when they anticipate an overbearing offensive. The fallacy that one must 'have it all together' before coming to Christ can be broken by expressing to those individuals the reality that we are all sinners, fallen short of perfection.

Disarming Strategy #4 – Show the Product Can Add Value

The 'value-added strategy' mirrors 'level the playing field' in that the intention is to show others that we're all trying to

---

[6] Romans 3:23 (NIV)

[7] Sanctification is being defined in this theological framework as the lifelong process by which we seek to achieve Christ-like holiness after the moment of initial salvation.

[8] Romans 12:3 (NIV)

muddle through the challenges of this life. It can seem awfully lonely at times, so at the end of the day a true sense of community is exactly the type of value most searching people are searching out. Community (in this case the Church / Body of Christ) is about contributing to a network of like-minded people beyond oneself: we will further delve into the value of the Church family in chapter four.

Much like other organizations that offer some type of product or service, the church must add value at every step throughout the ministry process and at every level of organizational leadership. This means that each and every organizational member, from the highest ranking executive to the part-time patron, must experience the intimate sense of community that is only present in the Body of Christ.

Adding value by creating community will be an exhausting and messy endeavor. Why? The only way to accomplish such a task is to build meaningful relationships with people. If this added-value is implemented, we will no longer be able to just show up at church and shake hands; we will now have to get as dirty as our savior did! Our new mantra will be 'love the unloved and befriend the social pariah.'

In the church adding value to the product or service will always be the difference between success and failure. The reality is that the church competes with numerous other value added products. Let's face it; there is plenty of external competition in the secular world biding for people's attention.

Synopsis

Marketing is a crucial component to the success of a church's ministry, and is often overlooked. There is no possible way that the church can do business without first being able to answer a few basic questions. By applying our mission as a church, we must try to find relevant ways to connect with people: in doing so we complete market research. Only can a church know the answer to that question after having asked a few subsequent ones: "Who are they? What do they want? How do they want it? When do they want it? Where do they want it? Why do they want it? What are their motivations? What are their unmet needs?

The last of the above questions, what are their unmet needs, is a point of struggle for many churches today. Leadership is quick to form useless, unattended programs and events that waste resources and create staff and volunteer frustration. Had the church initially asked this question, or any the others listed above, they would have realized that the very thing planned was completely irrelevant to those they were trying to reach. By making key determinations about market strategy early on, church's can waste less, devote greater resources to more effective ventures and essentially become an organization that operates leaner.

A Moment for Critical Thinking

1. Although the paper in the church office says 'saved' next to their name, have we ever considered what the Book of Life says? Have we adequately shown them the life-changing power of God's love?

2. What product is your church marketing? Are you marketing pure love in its rawest, Christ-like form?

3. Are you merely improving the esthetics because the product you've been offering is sub-par?

CHAPTER TWO

EMBRACING INNOVATION

Tradition

Anyone who has seen the movie "Fiddler on the Roof" (About a Jewish family in 1905 Russia) will probably be able to recite to you verbatim the scene of Tevye's song *Tradition*. I know this personally because my younger sister had an annoying habit of singing the movie's soundtrack over and over again when we were children.

In this iconic scene, Tevye expresses his desire that his eldest daughter Tzeitel marries the man which he has selected for her. This is so because it has always been done this way: it is tradition. However, Tzeitel has fallen deeply in love with another man: her childhood companion Motel the tailor. To the chagrin of her father Tzeitel inevitably gets her way and marries the tailor.

In the church, we create studies on how to increase Sunday school attendance or implement small groups. But maybe neither approach has meaning to the demographic that your church is designed to reach. When the Church holds to traditional methodology for the sake of avoiding change, it is nothing less than lazy. Still, the Church attempts to fit a square-peg ideology into a round-hole culture, and the problem isn't the round-hole.

In 1 Corinthians 9 the Apostle Paul writes: "I have become all things to all men so that by all possible means I might save some." In context, Paul is telling us that our purpose in this life is to be the kind of person that is willing to give up our own freedoms just to have the opportunity to be Christ in a meaningful way to someone else. In other words, we are to change our non-essential characteristics without compromising the integrity of our faith.

Change is today, and historically has been, a problem for the religious. The assumption is that we cannot alter the established church model for the sake of being relevant, and that somehow engaging in unconventional activities with hurting people will contaminate our souls. Oddly enough, Christianity is the dirtiest faith around. Scripture is laced with calls to feed the poor, clothe the naked and care for those who cannot care for themselves. Jesus knew that our interactions with the marginalized would be dirty, and I am fairly sure He celebrated that knowledge often.

The Prospect of Change

Change in the church, or the prospect of it, is an unavoidable reality confronting leadership and laity. In light of numerical growth and rapid environmental changes the local church is always being presented with opportunities to undergo a ministry shift that opposes its traditional methods, by introducing more culturally relevant ones. Altering the way that the local church interacts with its surrounding environment involves an understanding of how it identifies itself. Neatly hung posters of doctrinal statements on the wall and hymnals in the pew are reminders of a time when Christian ministry meant simplicity, but is it truly applicable to a spiritually hungry world today?

Adaptability

Within the church, the secular business world or any other competitor, your organization's adaptability will determine your chance for survival within its particular market niche. The church framework must continuously pursue innovation when it involves the way we relate to others. We accomplish this by keeping one ear to the existing people groups (the present congregation) and another ear to the future needs of the surrounding community: the potential congregation. Our relevance depends on its ability to continually learn from its cultural and demographic surroundings, while improving upon them. Understanding the dynamics of complex partnerships and competitive relationships is the cornerstone to effectively relating to a surrounding community. The church can be deemed ineffective when it is no longer relational.

Vision Casting

One tremendous challenge facing culturally irrelevant churches is the lack of foresight concerning the Church of tomorrow. Vision-casting is an art lost in the hustle of maintaining day-to-day operations of the facility, yet is crucial to the development of the localized body of believers. In the *Lead Pastor: CEO*[9] model, the senior leader of the church tends to often be the sole responsible party for vision-casting when it is truly meant to be a group effort.

Let's consider this scenario as though it were occurring in the secular business world. Most Fortune 500 companies have a number of directors that make executive decisions based upon the advisement of those below who carry out the day-to-day operations of the organization. Yet we expect a lead pastor alone to manage adequately the operations and vision-cast successfully? If we are truly honest with

---

[9] The *Lead Pastor: CEO* model is a description of an authoritarian rule of the local church by a senior or lead pastor.

ourselves, many Christians have been getting a free ride by compensating a senior leader to perform their share of Kingdom work.

 Being innovative involves looking at the successful organizations who evenly distribute power amongst those responsible for operations and at those who take the organization to the cutting-edge. Instead of the *Lead Pastor: CEO* model, might I propose we find a way to relinquish some control as leaders for the hope of becoming progressive? We must be courageous and innovative without compromising the quality of an unchanging message.

Sharing Information

 Some of the most effective and most fruitful ministries develop because senior church leadership has sought out best practices from leaders in the industry. More often than not, the senior leadership members of successful churches are willing to divulge their best ministry practices in hopes that other churches will flourish, build upon them and share best practices in return. In addition, each of us needs the support of one another as described in Galatians: "Carry each other's burdens, and in this way you will fulfill the law of Christ."[10]

 There are however some leaders unwilling to share information concerning successes: they essentially believe that their entire ministry is proprietary. These islands-unto-themselves churches eventually lack fresh innovation and

---

[10] Galatians 6:2 (NIV)

cease to grow in the same way that the networked churches do. Ministers who subscribe to a mindset of proprietary ministry may believe as though they are getting a jump on the competition, but they've missed that the greatest competitor of the church isn't itself; it's sin. In church ministry, one of the greatest resources for innovative success is an open relationship with peers. After all, it isn't our mission or church: it's God's!

    The Church stands today at a crossroad. We have an opportunity to innovate the way which we market God's love: you can be something meaningful to someone else by adapting without compromise. The only other option is to join Tevye and sing the praises of *Tradition*.

A Moment for Critical Thinking

1. As under shepherds, are we truly guarding the sheep from harm, or stunting their growth by insisting upon tradition?

2. Consider the Gospels. In what ways did Jesus celebrate the destruction of traditional things?

3. Are we adequately distributing power in the church so that vision-casting can occur?

4. How willing are we to network openly with other churches, sharing our success as well as our shortcomings?

SECTION TWO

LEADERSHIP

CHAPTER THREE

A LEADER WORTH FOLLOWING

The theory and practice of leading by first serving is foreign to many managers in our Western society. In contrast to a culture that seeks after self interests; the greatest emerging leader is one who is first a servant and only second a leader. Servant-leaders are people who are motivated by a natural desire to serve, who dream, who listen, who tolerate imperfection, who know the organizational goals and who has discovered the ultimate mission is serving the needs of others. This is not easily accomplished in corporate America where each individual is actively encouraged to rise above and edge-out his/her neighbor.

Despite what happens around us the Christian perspective should be drastically different, thus our actions in the workplace comparably different as well. Jesus said himself: "For even the Son of Man did not come to be served, but to serve and to give his life as a ransom for many."[11] Could there be any more perfect way to honor God than to model the leadership style of Jesus?

As I was sifting through familiar leaders of the past and present, I thought of a church board member named Leonard: he was the quintessential servant-leader. I will admit that Leonard is also a friend, so I have a slight bias toward his manner of conduct. Leonard, a man of compassion and empathy was trusted by nearly everyone in the congregation: his attitude fostered a climate of trust through his empathy. Tender-hearted Leonard heard and understood people's problems in a very organic way: he was a simple country fellow who related to people in a very natural way.

---

[11] Mark 10:45 (NIV)

I mention Leonard because so many organizational leaders have intentionally shied away from the servant-leader model due to some preconceived notion; a notion that service to those closest to the ground level will result in a eventual loss of authority. However, surrendering your managerial right to be powerful is liberating. When you concern yourself more with inspiring people and therefore managing generally on every organizational level, you free yourself from the managerial trap of micromanaging and earn a respect from the individuals you serve that you couldn't otherwise. The issues of power struggle are addressed further in chapters four and five.

A Moment for Critical Thinking

1. Consider your leadership style. How does it match up to the words of Jesus in Mark 10:45: "For even the Son of Man did not come to be served, but to serve and to give his life as a ransom for many."

2. Are you looking to gain something from your position in leadership or looking to give something to those you lead?

3. Is your desire to serve or be served?

CHAPTER FOUR

FINDING VALUE IN THE BODY

Gifts

I cannot recall where I heard this story, but I thought it would be a fitting prelude to this chapter. Although the only person a man usually shops for besides himself is that special lady in his life, the whole experience can be a stressful one. Many men have felt extremely frigid temperatures for long periods of time based on poor gift decisions, so this is a list of what not to buy.

1. Don't buy anything that plugs in. Anything that requires electricity is seen as too practical.

2. Don't buy clothing that involves sizes. The chances are one in seven thousand that you will get her size right, and she'll be offended the other 6999 times. Do I look like a size 16? she'll say. Too small a size doesn't cut it either: I haven't worn a size 2 in years!

3. Don't buy anything that involves weight loss or self-improvement. She'll perceive a six-month membership to the gym as a suggestion that's she's overweight, even though she's been talking about joining for the last year and a half.

4. Don't buy jewelry. The jewelry she really wants, you can't afford. And the jewelry you can afford, she doesn't want.

5. Finally, don't spend too much. How can you afford that? she'll ask. But don't spend too little. She won't say anything, but she'll think, Is that all I'm worth to this guy?

Although a complete volume of books should be written to guide men buying gifts, this chapter concerns the value of human capital within the Body of Christ. As for gifts, if you know that the gift is for you, the next thing you need to find out about a gift is who it came from; otherwise you'll look pretty stupid if you don't know who to credit the gift to:

> Now about spiritual gifts, brothers, I do not want you to be ignorant. You know that when you were pagans, somehow or other you were influenced and led astray to mute idols. Therefore I tell you that no one who is speaking by the Spirit of God says, "Jesus be cursed," and no one can say, "Jesus is Lord," except by the Holy Spirit.[12]

To understand what Paul is talking about in this passage, we should understand to whom he was speaking. The church at Corinth was fighting with a history of worshipping evil spirits, falling into idol worship and being oblivious to it all. Before Paul discusses the gifts of the Spirit in depth, he wants the church to be sure that they understand the difference between gifts of God and what is not of God. In the same way we're called to understand this, too. As we grow in Christ we must learn to recognize the difference between what is from God and what is not.

Not all of the gifts that are given are the same, and in fact, they're often going to vary from person to person.

> There are different kinds of gifts, but the same Spirit. There are different kinds of service, but the same Lord. There are different kinds of working, but the same God works all of them in all men. Now to each one the manifestation of the Spirit is given for the common good. To one there is given through the

---

[12] I Corinthians 12:1-3 (NIV)

> Spirit the message of wisdom, to another the message of knowledge by means of the same Spirit, to another faith by the same Spirit, to another gifts of healing by that one Spirit, to another miraculous powers, to another prophecy, to another distinguishing between spirits, to another speaking in different kinds of tongues, and to still another the interpretation of tongues.[13]

We don't always receive the same gift as the person next to us does, because each gift serves its own unique purpose. We simply don't all have the same personality traits or skill sets: you are different from me, and I am different from you. God created us and knows the extent of our abilities and knows how we can best be used. Furthermore, we don't all need the exact same gifts. On Christmas day do men get frilly dresses and makeup? No. Ladies, do you get power tools? Maybe, but chances are you don't. We don't all need the same gift to uplift ourselves or others in the body around us.

We're a family, making up the body of Christ. As a family we're bound together with love to do God's work here on Earth. We're charged to work together, each doing our individual part to help the body to function as a whole.

> All these are the work of one and the same Spirit, and he gives them to each one, just as he determines. The body is a unit, though it is made up of many parts; and though all its parts are many, they form one body. So it is with Christ. For we were all baptized by one Spirit into one body - whether Jews or Greeks, slave or free - and we were all given the

---

[13] 1 Corinthians 12:4-10 (NIV)

one Spirit to drink. Now the body is not made up of one part but of many.[14]

In this passage, Paul illustrates the use of the gifts by referencing the human body. Anyone who has taken a science class knows that the body is made up of many parts, all of them different and equally important. Despite their differences the body functions as one whole unit. In this passage we read the words "So it is with Christ," meaning so it is with Christ's body, the church. We are to function as one.

As we function as one the Spirit unites every believer in the Body, regardless of age, racial, economic or social status. We're all parts of the body of Christ, working together, and members of the family of God, loving and encouraging one another.

Being Family

I was always amazed as child at the intricacies of our Thanksgiving Day celebration. It was the biggest meal of the year for the family, and everyone knew exactly what dish that they were supposed to bring. My mother skillfully made the turkey (which my father would later carve); my grandmother made the dressing; my aunt was commissioned for the sweet potato casserole, and there were, of course, many other participants and dishes which aren't coming to my remembrance any longer.

The point of the Thanksgiving story is that without one particular dish being brought to the table, something about the meal would have been incomplete. Maybe the sweet potato casserole didn't get all of the publicity that the turkey

---

[14] 1 Corinthians 12:11-14 (NIV)

did, but it sure was missed last year when my aunt stopped making it. The same is so with the body of Christ:

> If the foot should say, "Because I am not a hand, I do not belong to the body," it would not for that reason cease to be part of the body. And if the ear should say, "Because I am not an eye, I do not belong to the body," it would not for that reason cease to be part of the body. If the whole body were an eye, where would the sense of hearing be? If the whole body were an ear, where would the sense of smell be? But in fact God has arranged the parts in the body, every one of them, just as he wanted them to be. If they were all one part, where would the body be? As it is, there are many parts, but one body.[15]

So how do we break down the gifts and church family, all with important roles, into the context of the churches we serve? I propose a few ideas:

Principle #1

Don't be envious of another part's job. Paul mentions in the above passage that regardless of what spiritual gift each person has, we can be certain that the Holy Spirit has distributed the gifts to produce His own results. No one should despise or be envious of another person's gift, because a gift given by the Spirit is for the good of all. He gave away the gifts as He saw fit.

Principle #2

Recognize your individual importance within the body. Scripture emphasizes how necessary it is to have diversity in a body for it to operate as one. Each part must be willing to

---

[15] 1 Corinthians 12:15-20 (NIV)

perform its own function and not seek to function in a role for which it was not made. The whole body can't be multiples of the same part or it wouldn't be a functioning body. It's the same way with the church. Members with one gift shouldn't deny that gift that they've been given and complain that they do not have some other gift. Again, no body can function as all eyes, all ears or all noses. So for the church to function properly it must have different gifts and different parts. It is God who has organized the body in the way that he wants it; remember that gifts are used for His glory, not ours!

Just as you grab hold to your importance in the body, realize how important your brothers and sisters in the body are as well: we really do need each other.

> The eye cannot say to the hand, "I don't need you!" And the head cannot say to the feet, "I don't need you!" On the contrary, those parts of the body that seem to be weaker are indispensable, and the parts that we think are less honorable we treat with special honor. And the parts that are unpresentable are treated with special modesty, while our presentable parts need no special treatment. But God has combined the members of the body and has given greater honor to the parts that lacked it, so that there should be no division in the body, but that its parts should have equal concern for each other.[16]

This bit of Scripture describes our dependence on the other members of the body. As the organs of the human body such as the eye, hand, head and feet need each other, so the members of the church with their various functions need each other too. Even the least attractive and hidden parts of the body are important and should be treated with

---

[16] 1 Corinthians 12:21-25 (NIV)

respect. This must be applied to the unseen and unnoticed members of our churches and greater communities at large as well.

It's not just the pastor or the worship band who get to outwardly show their gifts, but those who work behind the scenes like the people who set up and tear down the facilities, or those prayer warriors who sit quietly as they plead for their family and friends to know Christ. All must be assured of their value.

We need to value everyone, everyone's gifts, and everyone's contribution, because we're all in this together.

> If one part suffers, every part suffers with it; if one part is honored, every part rejoices with it. Now you are the body of Christ, and each one of you is a part of it.[17]

It's kind of like when one part of your body aches, it seems the rest joins in, or when your stomach is ill and your whole body seems to stop functioning just to come to the stomach's aid. As the body of Christ we must respond in kind. When one is hurting, we come to a brief, but screeching halt to aid the hurting member, or hurting part.

---

[17] 1 Corinthians 12:26-27 (NIV)

A Moment for Critical Thinking

1. As the body of Christ, are we truly valuing each part and each function equally?

2. As leaders, do we see the value of one's gifts as equal to our own, or do we view gifts given to us as more important?

CHAPTER FIVE

EMPOWERING PEOPLE

Stewardship of People

Non-profit organizations, churches in particular, must fully integrate the principles of stewardship. Beginning with our commitment to being accountable for something much greater than ourselves, we are accountable to the patrons for the way that we use organizational resources, whether they are the finances or an individual's abilities. In as much, ministry of any kind is a partnership in which everyone must have a say, but this partnership does not always mean that each member of the body will get exactly what he/she wants. It means that you may lose your argument, but you should never lose your voice.

As patrons across all demographics enter the Church, it is our Scriptural obligation to empower them to serve their Church body and community at large. Throughout the process, we have to trust that they can perform each task with only our guidance, not our constant critiques. Because we are stewards, control over ministry must be relinquished so that the laity may exercise and develop their God-given abilities. We cannot provide for every need, nor should we try to. The answer to is to empower patrons and they will be capable of ministering in whatever capacity they're asked to, using the unique gifts they've been given.

As the leadership, it is our duty to open the lines of communication for the suggestions and concerns of the greater body. We can't forget that in many cases they *asked* us to lead them; we're not entitled to do so. Our task is to ensure that when we step aside the organization still exists for the next generation. As a leader, the greatest thing you can do for the organization is to work your way out of a job. What an amazing accomplishment to say that the people working under you, become so empowered because of you, that they no longer needed you. That's the mark of a true leader!

Patrons must not depend on the security that we can provide them but be able to minister apart from the leadership team. If we care-take, we treat others, especially those in lower power positions, as if they were not able to provide for themselves. Not only will the patrons resent us for treating them like dependents, but we'll never know what they can accomplish in ministry without our constant supervision. The Apostle Paul discusses the dangers of poorly formed believers at length in 1 Corinthians 3.

Struggle for Power

All persons within the church play some role in its political processes, despite their small number. To understand the extent of power that each one holds, it may help to divide them into three groups: the pastoral leadership, the executive board, and the general population of patrons. Among these groups is an ongoing struggle for power.

The Pastor

More often than not, the local church is in conflict because patrons view the power of one leader as too absolute. While the majority of administrative power is given to the holder of that position, voting and non-voting patrons will often express their feelings of discontentment throughout the decision-making process. This occurs because the decisions that directly impact their lives are regularly being made without their voice being heard, thus creating dissension between those who make decisions and those who have to live with them.

Power within the church is distributed in a particular, systematic manner. The senior pastor is given a formal or legitimate authority to lead and direct the church in a way that he/she sees fit. Most administrative actions, liked or not, are justified because the church constitution grants the pastor the right to exercise a form of absolute power.

Chapter 2 introduced the leadership model employed by many present-day churches, referred to in this text as *Lead Pastor: CEO*. Still, I'm not entirely convinced that this is how it was meant to be.

> It was he who gave some to be apostles, some to be prophets, some to be evangelists, and some to be pastors and teachers, to prepare God's people for works of service, so that the body of Christ may be built up until we all reach unity in the faith and in the knowledge of the Son of God and become mature, attaining to the whole measure of the fullness of Christ.[18]

This is a very familiar passage where Paul describes the multi-fold ministry within the Church. Without diminishing the role of the pastor, I can't help but question the moment that we first embraced *Lead Pastor: CEO*. For many reasons, having a localized ministry (i.e. church) limited in scope by one fully compensated pastor seems counterproductive.

In no way am I implying that churches should end the pastor's pay, because Scripture is clear on that matter as well: "Do not defraud your neighbor or rob him. Do not hold

---

[18] Ephesians 4:11-13 (NIV)

back the wages of a hired man overnight."[19] What is being proposed here is a new model in which 'lateral' management is employed above the current 'top-down.'

The Board

The church board often acts as an extension of a frustrated congregation, and is likewise able to exercise little power. Even so, they are not exempt from conflict as they hold the keys to the church's finances. Pastoral staff initiatives are occasionally thwarted by the board denying the release of funding for them. Reversely, when the board approves funding that the larger congregation disapproves of, they are perceived to be disloyal to those they were elected to serve.

The board's source of power, and way in which it's used, is vastly different from the pastor's. Although their ability to create initiatives is limited, they aren't powerless. The board's greatest source of power comes from their ability to control and distribute organizational resources. In this way, they may opt to function as a counter organization by under-funding pastoral initiatives.

The Patrons

Finally, the primary source of power for voting congregants is their ability to elect pastors democratically and yearly elect board members to represent their specific interests. Depending on the church's constitution, they may also meet to approve or deny authorizations of spending for large projects; e.g., building or parking facilities. Beyond this point, there are very few initiatives or circumstances that

---

[19] Leviticus 19:13 (NIV)

would require participation of the voting members of the congregation.

Empowering People

Conflict between leadership and laity can surface when laity is told that they're a functional part of the church at annual business meetings, yet are given little opportunity to make decisions throughout the year that guide the church's overall development. If people are to remain grafted into the church body, they must be empowered to serve their church and local community. Once the leadership relinquishes their autocratic control over ministry, others can exercise and develop their own abilities.

The congregants must not depend on the security that the pastoral staff can provide to them but be able to minister autonomously of the leadership team. If we spoon-feed the basics of faith and ministry to these congregants weekly, as though they don't already know them: we proceed to show a significant lack of trust. In doing so, the congregation could easily resent the leadership for treating them like dependents, and we'll never know what they can accomplish in ministry without constant supervision.

A Moment for Critical Thinking

1. What are you doing as a leader to empower the people you serve?

2. What type of conflict can you recognize in your own church body?

3. Is your local church following the *Lead Pastor: CEO* model, or do you practice lateral leadership?

Section Three

Operations

CHAPTER SIX

ORGANIZATIONAL CULTURES

Understanding Organizational Subcultures

All organizations foster a culture - intentionally or not. Segments of the larger organization mirror unique subcultures within the parent organization; this you likely know. However, my fear is that the environment created in many franchises gives active participants an unfortunate picture of the parent organization, providing the subculture is truly to be a mirror of it. Churches, your parent organization is the body of Christ, regardless of denominational affiliation.

Daily, our participants are expected to fight battles on multiple fronts. They vigorously contend with the demands of a tough work environment, family, and the increasingly complex expectations set forth by an often out-of-touch church framework. We as leaders often work our most willing participants to the point of exhaustion without attempting to develop them professionally.

In the context of any organization, people are the greatest asset. We must ask the question though, are these people assets that we can anticipate a long-term return on, or are they assets merely placed in a no yield savings account?

I've personally been employed by organizations that we're content to hold me where I was, and many organizations adhere to that model. However, if participants on all levels are not given opportunities for growth or advancement (i.e. promotions or special projects) they will eventually become bored and find an organization that embraces their creative abilities. Organizations mustn't let the focus become one-sided, being more concerned with maintaining daily operations than long-term growth.

Have you considered that the environment in which we have created within the church for our patrons to work might be toxic? If we're honest, morale is low and small communities of participants are hurting. We're all human, desiring honesty, compassion and a complete understanding of our most basic human needs. Therefore, our response as leaders must be organic, and deeply rooted in a desire to serve.

I am reminded of a scene in the popular 2000 movie *Remember the Titans,* when high school football team captain Gerry Bertier tells teammate Julius Campbell, "That's the worst attitude ever." In turn, Julius responds, "Attitude reflects leadership, captain." If we seek a reason for why the people of the organization we lead have a bad attitude, we need not look any further than the mirror.

Conflict

Conflict within the church organization almost always has a negative connotation attached to it. This stems from a history of heated debates over items of little consequence, such as contemporary vs. traditional song services, the color of fabric on the pews, and how the pastor was to be clothed as he delivered the morning sermon. Although positions on the inconsequential issues lack the merit of other more important ones, there is no doubt that interests worth hearing are involved because there are people involved.

Conflict is unavoidable; whether it arises in a church setting or not. Wherever there are two or more opposing arguments, conflict will arise, but how we manage the conflict is up to us. As the Body of Christ, is our duty to handle disagreements in a Christ-like manner, not to be a person forcing their will upon others.

Organizational Culture, Social Norms and Conflict

An organization like a church deals with conflict in a uniquely passive way, much like that of compromise. As issues of conflict within the church surface, congregants, board members, and church staff have a tendency to concede their lightly taken position to others, simply for the sake of keeping the peace. Unfortunately, the people's passivity also creates an opportunity the dominant few in the church to consistently have their way or assert their will on the passive majority.

Dealing with Conflict

Dealing with conflict in the church can be a challenging task. Thankfully the Word of God contains a number of principles for managing such situations.

Do not let time pass

Allowing significant time to pass after the initial moment of conflict will only deepen the anger stirring within. Thus, "In your anger do not sin: Do not let the sun go down while you are still angry."[20]

Paul isn't speaking here of a righteous indignation but of a bitterness that can lead to sin. We know that conflict is inevitable: you cannot control whether or not it happens. What you can control is how it plays out in the church.

---

[20] Ephesians 4:26 (NIV)

I've reflected often on this passage as I think about the first church I pastored. As wonderful as the experience was, the lead pastor and I didn't get along very well: there was unaddressed conflict that lead to the eventual deterioration of our relationship. As I became increasingly frustrated with the situation, I harbored the bitterness and anger, declining God's nudging to reopen the lines of communication. Neither of us took the initiative to resolve the conflict, and it became a dim spot in my life of ministry to God and others. Don't allow conflict to harm your ministry.

Make resolution a priority

In addition to the resolution of conflict being timely, it must come as a spiritual priority. In fact, the very act of ignoring this principle can create a barrier in our worship to God. Jesus offers this advice:

> "Therefore, if you are offering your gift at the altar and there remember that your brother has something against you; leave your gift there in front of the altar. First go and be reconciled to your brother; then come and offer your gift. Settle matters quickly with your adversary who is taking you to court. Do it while you are still with him on the way, or he may hand you over to the judge, and the judge may hand you over to the officer, and you may be thrown into prison."[21]

No matter what place of ministry that we find ourselves in, allowing unresolved conflict to fester within can severely stunt the growth of our relationship with Christ and others. Throughout the course of this chapter, we touched a number of times on the importance of managing conflict appropriately, because we certainly cannot avoid it.

---

[21] Matthew 5:23-24 (NIV)

A Moment for Critical Thinking

1. What is the attitude in your organization?

2. Is the attitude a reflection of your leadership?

3. How does your organization deal with conflict?

4. Do you have any unresolved conflict with your brothers and sisters in Christ?

CHAPTER SEVEN

STEWARDSHIP

In previous chapters, we discussed stewardship of our greatest resource: people. Now, in our pursuit of a holistic perspective, we forge onward by exploring the stewardship of organizational resources unrelated to human capital. In the next few pages we'll outline the Scriptural guidelines regarding spending and care for the poor. Our job will be to build a working model that allows a Judeo-Christian society to consume, without neglecting its ethical duties.

Budgeting

Let's consider the concept of budgeting organizational finances. Although some feel it's a time wasted, budgeting supports the vision of the organization and is the tangible evidence of a vision. Vision is crucial because Proverbs 29:18a in the KJV states: "Where there is no vision, the people perish."

Beyond vision-casting, budgeting compels the church to declare its primary goals as an organization, and assess its priorities. Many sermons have been delivered from ivory pulpits using this cliché to push the agenda for personal giving: "Look at the expenses in your checkbook register, and there your heart is."

> "Sell your possessions and give to the poor. Provide purses for yourselves that will not wear out, a treasure in heaven that will not be exhausted, where no thief comes near and no moth destroys. For where your treasure is, there your heart will be also."[22]

---

[22] Luke 12:33-34 (NIV)

The practice of budgeting also promotes an acute awareness of organizational finances; in the church, we call it stewardship. There can be useful, planned expenditures, provided they're proportionate to reasonable projected income and resources in reserve, and prioritized by order of necessity.

Finally, budgeting provides a means for accountability. It curtails unethical financial practices (i.e. embezzlement, avoiding taxes, etc.) and prevents dictatorial spending practices. When there is a solid budget in place, no one person (i.e. pastor or board) is the immediate or uncontested authority in church spending.

The Global Church

The church is a prime example of an institution put into direct contact with a global economy and many marginalized people groups. So what are we doing to care for these particular people with the resources we have? Many functional programs, such as soup kitchens, clothing drives, free clinics, charity hospitals, and bill-helps are already in place to assist the poor (resource-takers) with obtaining goods and services that they would otherwise not receive. More churches should, however, being doing more. Unfortunately the ratio of freely-giving church people to poor resource-takers is not in favor of the church being able to reach everyone. Still, I must wonder if socially oriented government programs would have been developed the church was functioning as designed?

God has a very clear plan of how His people (the Church) should be doing business. With good stewardship, individuals contribute a portion of the resources with which they've been entrusted to the Church (Body of Christ) as mandated by Scripture. Through the Church (Body of Christ) God not only takes care of the marginalized but expands the trust of the contributor. This shouldn't be confused with a health-and-wealth Gospel, but used instead to develop an understanding that God cares for the needs of all His people, and uses members of the body to meet basic needs.

Consumerism

Western society has encouraged its citizens to continuously consume; even in the light of the growing number of impoverished around us. When our resources (in this context: assets) have been depleted, our desire for uninterrupted over-consumption causes us to turn to consumer credit to maintain lifestyles that we cannot afford. The pitfalls of excessive debt are for another time and another place though.

Consumerism isn't a new practice: mankind has been consuming since time began, when ancient tribes bartered in shells and obsidian flakes for hides and dried meat. Consumption has historically driven empires to the heights of power and to the point of destruction as the desire to consume drove excessive pursuits. To this end, royal greed drove many kingdoms and empires to the point of excessive consumption.

Today we live in a society saturated with consumer options and drives; we have more choices than we know what to do with! We're constantly compelled to buy, but how ethical is the ideology of consumerism? In other words, how ethical is it for us to consume to a point where it becomes who and what we are as a society? Should we allow consumerism to define us?

Although consumerism is not confined to the market culture of the United States, the ideology of consumerism is very prevalent in our culture. Some argue that consumerism is an ideology where consumption has become a moral good. As consumers, it's simply good to consume. In this model, a person's life is molded by an industry of good and bad being based on whether or not one is consuming at the normative level that society has generated.

Culture saturated with the ideology of consumerism has taken the act of reasonable consumption and turned it into a desire for lavish living. It tends to happen, then, that the individuals of the society judge their world by it; they must have more than their neighbor does. Consequently, their perception of superiority or inferiority is based on this comparison. If we allow, this ideology of consumerism can become the filter, or lens, through which many social issues are viewed. Through this lens, we can easily lose sight of the poor.

The Poor & Marginalized

As we who have disposable cash and open credit consume, one must wonder about those who have neither of those resources. Furthermore, as we consume to satisfy our superficial needs, do we consider the poor who have no access to those goods? Is it right that we indulge in excess, while there are those in need of the most basic of life's things?

The Bible provides a foundation for the care of the poor. Throughout both the Old and New Testaments, care for the poor is a recurring theme; the needy are mentioned in various ways. Old Testament Scriptures mention three distinct Hebrew terms for the needy, each with their distinct meaning and implications for the concern shown to them by God.

Appearing throughout the Old Testament, often wherever the less fortunate are mentioned, is the Hebrew word *Ebyown*. Its meaning relates to one that is in want, needy, chiefly poor, subject to oppression and abuse, needing deliverance from trouble: especially as delivered by God, and generally references the lowest class of people. These people, or *Ebyown*, depended completely on others for their survival. As the poor often are, the *Ebyown* were often preyed upon by others seeking personal gain. A prime example of the *Ebyown* can be found in the book of Deuteronomy:

> There will always be poor people in the land. Therefore I command you to be openhanded toward your brothers and toward the poor and needy in your land.[23]

In this passage, God tells his people that the matter of the needy will always be there. His command to His people states that they should freely share with their needy peers as well as the poor around them. Yahweh is placing great importance on how His people assist with the survival of the *Ebyown*, speaking of how He wants this sharing to be done - with an open heart and with no thought as to how it will economically affect the giver.

---

[23] Deuteronomy 15:11 (NIV)

Another Old Testament classification for the poor is *Aniy*. Its meaning references the poor, afflicted, humble, wretched, needy, and weak. The *Aniy* of Scripture can be found in Deuteronomy 24:10-15:

> When you make a loan of any kind to your neighbor, do not go into his house to get what he is offering as a pledge. Stay outside and let the man to whom you are making the loan bring the pledge out to you. If the man is poor, do not go to sleep with his pledge in your possession. Return his cloak to him by sunset so that he may sleep in it. Then he will thank you, and it will be regarded as a righteous act in the sight of the LORD your God. Do not take advantage of a hired man who is poor and needy, whether he is a brother Israelite or an alien living in one of your towns. Pay him his wages each day before sunset, because he is poor and is counting on it. Otherwise he may cry to the LORD against you, and you will be guilty of sin.[24]

Here the poor and needy are those who need protection from employers and creditors. God goes to great lengths to portray his desire that his people help the poor - those without personal resources and wealth of any sort - even if the *Aniy* were employees or debtors. In verse fifteen God warns the employer of the poor that the mistreatment of his *Aniy* employees will be seen as a sin. The modern application can be quickly related to the usury of which many creditors have been accused.

We can find another example of Aniy in the Psalms. A quick glimpse at our theme in the psalmist's declaration reveals that God sees the injustice of the needy and will rescue them. "But the needy will not always be forgotten, nor

---
[24] Deuteronomy 24:10-15 (NIV)

the hope of the afflicted ever perish."[25] The evidence supporting the concern for the needy as a thematic element to the Old Testament mounts in a later passage. God declares that He has heard the groaning of the Aniy and the oppression of the needy.

> Because of the oppression of the weak and the groaning of the needy, I will now arise," says the LORD. "I will protect them from those who malign them.[26]

The final Hebrew term that we will explore in regard to the poor is *Dal*. Its meaning refers to one who is low, poor, weak, or thin. This type of needy references those who lacked a voice. Dal was often used to refer to poor peasant farmers whose poverty level had stripped them of any social status in their day and left them without any type of societal clout. An example of Dal can be found in Isaiah 10:

> Woe to those who make unjust laws, to those who issue oppressive decrees, to deprive the poor of their rights and withhold justice from the oppressed of my people, making widows their prey and robbing the fatherless. What will you do on the day of reckoning, when disaster comes from afar? To whom will you run for help? Where will you leave your riches?[27]

In this passage we find that the prophet Isaiah is expressing the anger of the Lord against Israel, and those who were oppressing the needy through unjust laws and decrees. Isaiah is expressing God's displeasure over the fact that those in charge of making the nation's laws are using them to deprive the poor (*Dal*) of their rights and render them

---

[25] Psalm 9:18 (NIV)
[26] Psalm 12:5 (NIV)
[27] Isaiah 10:1-3 (NIV)

helpless. This use of *Dal* illustrates the Old Testament concern of a God who cares both for the financially destitute and society's oppressed.

Ethics

Old Testament ethics, both in general and with regard to the poor, are a reflection of the character of God because morals and faith in the Old Testament were inseparably linked. Both morals and the Law began with a healthy fear of Yahweh and reflected the way that the people of God perceived His character. As a result, God's mandates toward the care of the poor were both a matter of faith and Law. Following God's laws concerning care for the poor meant that the Israelites were reflecting the nature of their God. This personal interest in the needy amongst His worshippers set the Israelites apart from other societies. Such similarities exist in New Testament times with Christian duties to the body of Christ.

Inequalities in human life were exhibited everywhere in the Old Testament world and there was no lack of those who deliberately took advantage of the *Ebyown*, *Aniy*, and the *Dal*. What made Israel different was that it accepted that it was the object of affection to a loving God who insisted that the welfare of even the lowliest of persons was of utmost importance.

The last piece of this overarching theme is the responsibility that the rich ("heavy consumers") had towards the poor.

> If there is a poor man among your brothers in any of the towns of the land that the LORD your God is giving you,

do not be hardhearted or tightfisted toward your poor brother. Rather be openhanded and freely lend him whatever he needs.[28]

People of affluence were expected to recognize their duty to lend a hand towards those in need. It was not enough that they acknowledged that the poor had a place before their God; they also had to reach down and loosen their purse strings. The wealthy, as well as all other Israelites, had a duty towards God, and through Him to all those around them, including the poor and oppressed. Their responsibilities and duties toward Yahweh included their duties towards the poor.

There is a foundation for the Old Testament mandate of caring for the needy. Israel was a nation that belonged to and dwelled in their God. The very land that they lived in was not their own but the property of God. He gave to them freely and expected the same behavior out of each child, notwithstanding rank, title, or economic status.

Synopsis

As capitalists we delight ourselves in the benefits of an open market. This resource-taking option allows every individual to strive for a personal best: the opportunity to obtain great wealth. Capitalists love the idea that the playing field is wide, open, and filled with opportunities for success and wealth on a grand scale. However, very few ever achieve such grandeur of wealth. Quietly amongst the wealthy and middle class abide the marginalized of society. The marginalized peoples are those who either weren't

---

[28] Deuteronomy 15:7-8 (NIV)

successful in their efforts to play the resource-taking game, or they're unable to do so.

Consumerism is a natural part of life, but like anything is appropriate when taken in moderation. Our consumer-driven, capitalist society should instead be viewed as a voluntary system of human relationships which has been constructed for the goal of mutual exchange. However, it is our duty to protect it with laws that prohibit fraud, unjust force and theft. In fact, capitalism holds several basic conditions which must be held to in order for its framework of voluntary market relations to exist.

The underlying principle of capitalism is, in fact, that of basic human rights: such as the right to make decisions, the right to freedom, the right to hold property and the right to exchange one's own property for that of another. It also encourages the development of important social virtues, such as community and cooperation.

Judeo-Christian ethics and capitalism don't always have to mean conflict when they meet. Having tied the ideology of consumerism to our perception of social responsibilities, we should ask ourselves the question: "In what way does the ideology of consumerism conflict with the ethics of the Bible?"

If society is not careful, the ideology of consumerism will tell us that as long as we are meeting our society's generated normative level of consumption, that we are fulfilling our ethical duties. This very statement excludes the poor. If we exalt consumerism and place prominence of morality based on market affluence, then we violate the Judeo-Christian ethic of care for the poor. Again, we must build a working model that allows a Judeo-Christian society to consume, without neglecting its ethical duties. Western ideology and practice must include care for the poor, in spite of rampant consumerism. Many in our world are growing more destitute and distant from us by the day, while select populations grow wealthier amidst the suffering of the less fortunate. The practice of caring is a not just a matter for the governments of our day to handle. Just as the people of Israel realized that it was their responsibility to see to the care of the poor, the contemporary Church must rise to that example.

Our ideology of consumerism is viewed through the filter of western culture. Judeo-Christian ethics conflict with the ideology of extreme consumerism. The Old and New Testament authors spoke truth in a way that calls for us to care for the needy and consume less. Society cannot fulfill the ethic of care for the poor if they are only following the structural ethics of the ideology of consumerism. We must adhere to an ethic that views our duties through a theological lens that is firmly planted in a concern for the poor.

A Moment for Critical Thinking

1. We as ministers are often quick to burden our sheep on the individual level, but when it comes to organizational spending, do we approach it with the same scrutiny.

2. Are churches truly advocating social justice through feeding the hungry, clothing the naked and sheltering the homeless?

3. Are we caring for the orphans and widows, or are we more intent on spending our limited resources remodeling the church lobby and hiring an extra staff member?

4. How ethical is consumption in light of the poor, and how ethical is consumption when driven by consumer credit?

5. What should we do with the marginalized peoples of society?

CHAPTER EIGHT

A FREELY GIVING CHURCH

In the previous chapter we explored the nuances of stewardship. In this chapter we will discuss how it can specifically apply to the church. Might I suggest that churches, much like individuals, could be categorized in two ways: miserly or freely giving.

The Miserly

The earthly ministry of Jesus is bursting with meetings between the Lord of all creation and people seeking after something greater. It is in Matthew's Gospel that we encounter a prime example of the miserly, more commonly known to us as the rich young ruler.

> Just then a man came up to Jesus and asked, "Teacher, what good thing must I do to get eternal life?" "Why do you ask me about what is good?" Jesus replied. "There is only one who is good. If you want to enter life, keep the commandments." "Which ones?" he inquired. Jesus replied, "You shall not murder, you shall not commit adultery, you shall not steal, you shall not give false testimony, honor your father and mother," and 'love your neighbor as yourself." "All these I have kept," the young man said. "What do I still lack?" Jesus answered, "If you want to be perfect, go, sell your possessions and give to the poor, and you will have treasure in heaven. Then come, follow me." When the young man heard this, he went away sad, because he had great wealth. Then Jesus said to his disciples, "Truly I tell you, it is hard for someone who is rich to enter the kingdom of heaven. Again I tell you, it is easier for a camel to go through the

eye of a needle than for someone who is rich to enter the kingdom of God."[29]

In this familiar story we see a man who knows and keeps the Law, much like many present-day churchgoers. Although, if we use the Gospels as a template for living (and it seems wise that we do), it's abundantly clear that Jesus was never satisfied with merely keeping the Law: He always set the bar higher. In fact, His very statement "If you want to be perfect" tells the listener that the previously mentioned criteria (the keeping of the Law) is somehow lacking in the light of surrendering everything for the sake of the call.

Jesus offers our rich young ruler an opportunity to wholeheartedly serve Him, but it could only come at a significant cost. He clearly understands what Jesus' imperative means: sell it all, give it all away, and then you'll be my follower. It's only then that we see one of the most heartbreaking moments in Scripture: our rich young ruler, now nothing more than a miser, walks away from his creator because his wealth is what truly has ownership of his heart.

The defining character flaw that plunges our rich young ruler into the category of miser was his inability to balance earthly and heavenly riches. It's a characteristic whose application easily transfers to present-day churches. Yes, if we are truly honest with ourselves, our churches could be doing so much more to be advocates for those in our surrounding communities.

---

[29] Matthew 19:16-24 (NIV)

The Freely Giving

Movie buffs might recall the biography of German businessman Oskar Schindler, as depicted in the 1993 film Schindler's List. In this masterful work of cinematography, Schindler was credited with saving more than one thousand Polish-Jews during the holocaust by granting them employment, although his intentions didn't start so nobly. Through an intermediate, profit-hungry Schindler acquired a workforce primarily made up of Jews because of the low wages they were to receive in exchange for their work. However, his heart was broken after seeing the senseless killing of innocent people, and he gave the SS a handsome bribe for each worker he listed as necessary for the operations of his factory. In doing so, he kept them from certain death at Nazi hands.

As the story comes to a close, Schindler parted ways with his workers, being moved in a deeply profound way. As he observed his surroundings, he considered what else he could have sold just to save "one more life." Oskar Schindler witnessed injustice and gave all he had to give, just to save a life. Oskar Schindler and the rich young ruler represent opposite ends of the giving spectrum. At this point ask yourself the question, "which end of the spectrum am I closer to?"

A Different Direction

If we are to truly become the church that Christ intended for us to be, then we must take intentional steps to move from miserly to giving. It is simply not enough to offer a prayer for the hungry to be fed, when you hold a bounty of food in your hand. It is simply not enough to plead with God for at-risk youth to make right choices, when you have the influence to show them how to live. It is simply not enough to pray for world peace, when Jesus says, "Blessed are the peacemakers, for they will be called sons of God."[30]

    As a church (collective group of Christ's followers), we must act like an army of Schindlers. As I thought of how to capture this in words, the only thing that came to mind was micro-stewardship. The thought behind micro-stewardship is that the church be held accountable for every penny spent. I'm not saying that the church should not have nice things or improve the building's facade, but when it occurs as a priority over feeding the hungry, clothing the naked, giving to the poor, or sheltering the widow and orphan, a grave injustice is done. If we truly adopted micro-stewardship, we would see every penny of church resources not as a way to re-carpet the year old sanctuary, but we would see it as the hot meal and cozy blanket that pulls the unsaved homeless man from the brink of eternity.

---

[30] Matthew 5:9 (NIV)

A Moment for Critical Thinking

1. Look internally first: are you a "rich young ruler" or an Oskar Schindler?

2. Now examine your organization (church); is it a "giving" body or a "miserly" one?

3. What would micro-stewardship look like in your local congregation?

CHAPTER NINE

AN ORGANIZATION RE-MADE

Redesigning the Body

When all attempts to modify the existing infrastructure have failed, organizations need to be completely redesigned. Many church organizations fail to perform adequately due to aging processes beyond mere repair. Failing operations, greater competition and a lesser quality product presentation have surfaced the notion that if the church doesn't somehow change, it will lose much of its influence. In short, we must redesign the church's ministry to look like that of Jesus. I hope it is evident that the purpose of this book: *In Jesus' Briefcase* is to point us (as the body of Christ) to Scripture when we try to grasp for solutions on how to handle the business of the Church.

The primary component of organization, the operational mission, often fails to coincide with the actual activities of the church. Many bodies have either forgotten, or strayed from their original reason-for-being. In response, we must create a culture of ministry based on a set of Biblical values that applies to the community we serve. In doing so, we will define the church's operational mission and revitalize its drive its success. Beginning with the mission of the church, then through many other aspects of operations, common business principles are often avoided by the leadership. However, it's imperative that church leadership embraces the reality that God and business can and should coexist.

Appealing to a new generation of 'church' consumers involves more than a few cosmetic upgrades in processes, but an entire sift in approach: or a reengineering of the organizational processes: we touched on this in chapter one. To be effective, churches must eliminate traditional methods and embrace a redesign that will alter the way people consume the 'church' product.

Proposed Operations

One way to determine whether or not the church's operations deliver more value than the competition is to use benchmarking. Benchmarking involves being humble enough to study other organizations, employ new methodologies to the ministry and set the church's goals toward the best in the industry. Much like in the for-profit environment, which tends to exchange information more freely than religious non-profits, churches must be both humble and open enough to freely share best demonstrated practices and failures: another issue previously addressed in chapter two.

The church must work toward a continuous improvement of its many systems. Starting with purpose, we must sustain it at all cost by keeping the focus on attaining consistent outcomes, and improved services and programs. Second, leadership happens when management: the board and pastoral staff, models the way that the church must go and sets all expectations accordingly. Third, teamwork is implementable when all members of the church enter into an equal partnership with one another. Fourth, consumer relationships are developed when we understand and hear the heartbeat of the community which we are called to serve. Lastly, and what I believe to be most important to the success of the church: people must be empowered. Teach church members, volunteers, and staff at all levels to function as the true body of Christ.

Synopsis

There is so much more at stake in a church's operational shift than potential giving increases: we're not in this for the money. Even with limited resources, churches must be good stewards of what they have and stay as lean as possible, while maximizing effectiveness. Striving for top quality, exercising good marketing strategies, maintaining innovation, retaining the best people, and continually adding value to the process and the products are all key components that every church must implement consistently. Those that are not – they must be redesigned.

A Moment for Critical Thinking

1. As you've read through this text, consider the state of your church and ask the questions

    a. What do our marketing strategies say about us?

    b. How are we leading: like stewards, or selfishly?

    c. What do our church's operations look like?

2. After everything is considered, is it time for your church to reengineer?

APPENDICIES

APPENDIX A

Recommended Resources and Selected Bibliography

Anderson, Matt. (2011). *Weekend With God.* Cleveland, Ohio: Createspeace.com.

Babbes, George S. and Zigarelli, Michael. (2006). *The Minister's MBA.* Nashville, Tennessee: B & H Publishing Group.

Blanchard, Ken and Hodges, Phil. (2005). *Lead Like Jesus.* Nashville, Tennessee: W Publishing Group.

Block, P.M (1993). *Stewardship.* San Francisco, CA: Berrett-Koehler Publishers.

Boyatzis, Richard; Goleman, Daniel and McKee, Annie. (2002). *Primal Leadership.* Boston, MA: Harvard Business School Press.

Clark, David K. and Robert V. Rakestraw, ed. (1996). Readings in Christian Ethics: Volume 2, Issues and Applications. Grand Rapids, MI: Baker Book House.

Creps, Earl. (2006). *Off Road Disciplines: Spiritual Adventures of Missional Leaders.* San Francisco, CA: Jossey-Bass.

Fitz-enz, Jac. (2000). *The ROI of Human Capital.* New York, NY: American Management Association.

Frost, Michael and Hirsch, Alan (2003). *The Shaping of Things to Come: Innovation and Mission for the 21st Century Church.* Peabody, MA: Hendrickson Publishers.

Greenleaf, R.K. (1977). *Servant Leadership.* New York, NY: Paulist Press.

Grenz, Stanley. (1996). *A Primer on Postmodernism.* Grand Rapids, MI: William B. Eerdmans Publishing Company.

Hirsch, Alan. (2006). *The Forgotten Ways.* Grand Rapids, MI: Brazos Press.

Kaiser, Walter C., Jr. (1983). *Toward Old Testament Ethics.* Grand Rapids, MI: Zondervan Publishing House.

Mounce, William D. ed. *The NIV English-Greek New Testament: A Reverse Interlinear: New International Version.* Grand Rapids, Michigan: Zondervan Publishing House, 1991.

Shepherd, David R. ed. *The Bible: The New Living Translation.* Nashville, Tennessee: Holman Bible Publishers Inc., 1996.

VanGemeren, Willem. "36 (ebyon)" In *New International Dictionary of Old Testament Theology and Exegesis*, Edited by Willem VanGemerem, Volume 1:228-232. Grand Rapids, Michigan: Zondervan, 1986.

VanGemeren, Willem. "1924 (dal)" In *New International Dictionary of Old Testament Theology and Exegesis*, Edited by Willem VanGemerem, Volume 1:946-947. Grand Rapids, Michigan: Zondervan, 1986.

VanGemeren, Willem. "6714 (aniy)" In *New International Dictionary of Old Testament Theology and Exegesis*, Edited by Willem VanGemerem, Volume 3:454-464. Grand Rapids, Michigan: Zondervan, 1986.

Zigarelli, Michael. (2006). *Christianity 9 to 5*. Kansas City, MO: Beacon Hill Press of Kansas City.

Scripture taken from the HOLY BIBLE, NEW INTERNATIONAL VERSION. Copyright 1973, 1978, 1984, 2011 by International Bible Society. Used by permission of Zondervan Bible Publishers.

www.word-solutions.com

www.agapetremont.com

www.inletdance.org

www.mattandersononline.com

www.lonjordan.net

www.earlcreps.com

www.360church.net

www.villagehouston.net

www.churchstaffing.com

APPENDIX B

Glossary of Terms

Contextualizing the Gospel Message: Refers to a process through which the message is communicated to an audience (large or small) by using social practices and language they would understand and use daily.

Lead Pastor CEO: A management model that describes the authoritarian rule of the local church by a senior or lead pastor.

Micro-Stewardship: Stewardship to the point which the church is held accountable for every penny spent, and every human resource used.

Miserly: The description of a person (or in this text people) who are very stingy with their resources.

Sanctification: Defined in this theological framework as the lifelong process by which we seek to achieve Christ-like holiness after the moment of initial salvation.

Vision Casting: The process of an organization planning for the future, inasmuch as Scripture permits.

About the Author

In college Stephen earned a B.S. in Chemistry from Lake Erie College ('02), a M.A. in Theological Studies from the Assemblies of God Theological Seminary ('06), and a MBA from Bluffton University ('09). He is also a licensed minister through Agape Inc.

Throughout his working years he's had the pleasure to serve God in various forums. Following the two years spent as the Assistant Pastor of an Ohio Assemblies of God Church, he moved back home where he took a position as an analyst at the nation's largest bank as well as partnered to plant Agape Inc (a non-denominational church in the Tremont neighborhood of Cleveland). Now Stephen has the distinguished privilege of teaching as an Adjunct Professor in the School of Business and Leadership at Malone University in Canton, Ohio.